TEA

BY VELINA HASU HOUSTON

D1235176

★

DRAMATISTS
PLAY SERVICE
INC.

TEA
Copyright © 2007, Velina Hasu Houston

All Rights Reserved

SPECIAL NOTE

SPECIAL NOTE ON SONGS AND RECORDINGS

TEA received its world premiere at Manhattan Theatre Club (Lynne Meadow, Artistic Director; Barry Grove, Managing Director) in New York City on October 6, 1987. It was directed by Julianne Boyd. The set design was by Wing Lee; the costume design was by C.L. Hundley; the lighting design was by Greg MacPherson; the sound design was by Bruce Ellman; and the stage manager was Renee Lutz. The cast was as follows:

ATSUKO YAMAMOTO .... Natsuko Ohama
SETSUKO BANKS .... Takayo Fischer
TERUKO MACKENZIE .... Lily Mariye
HIMIKO HAMILTON .... Patti Yasutake
CHIZUYE JUAREZ .... Jeanne Mori

TEA was subsequently produced at the Old Globe Theatre in San Diego, California; Pittsburgh Public Theatre in Pittsburgh, Pennsylvania; A Contemporary Theatre in Seattle, Washington; Whole Theatre in Montclair, New Jersey; and at other theatres in the U.S. and internationally.

CHARACTERS

ATSUKO YAMAMOTO
SETSUKO BANKS
TERUKO MACKENZIE
HIMIKO HAMILTON
CHIZUYE JUAREZ

NOTE: This play is to be performed without an intermission. Average running time is eighty-five minutes.

TEA

Prelude

Invitation to Tea

In the darkness, a, female American voice belts out "God Bless America." A quiet, traditional Japanese melody — perhaps "Sakura" — cuts into the song's end as lights reveal a netherworld. Enter Himiko, a pale, delicately-boned woman wearing a feminine, mysterious dress [its little-girlishness and antiquity suggest a different era]; a white petticoat with shredded hems hangs underneath. Over the dress is a distorted kimono. Himiko relates to an unseen presence. She is beautiful, but beaten; and exudes an aura of sultry mystery. There is no lunacy in this woman, rather the sense of one who has been pushed to the edge, tried desperately to hold on, and failed. She is, indeed, resolute. Himiko reaches out to the presence.

HIMIKO. Billy. Can't you see it's me? Himiko Hamilton. You gave me your name and, this day, I give it back. You have forsaken my spirit and it stands shaking in the cold mist left behind by your restless breath. As you walk. Fast. And always away. Leaving me to wander between two worlds forever. *(A quiet smile appears.)* But listen, Billy, listen. I have learned your Christian prayer "Now I lay me down to sleep. I pray your Lord my soul to keep. And if I die before I wake. I pray your Lord my soul to take." *(Attention is suddenly drawn to another presence which absolutely delights her; she moves toward it slightly.)* Mieko-chan? This is your mother. Come close. Let me smell the confusion of your Amerasian skin. For you are the only gift I ever had. Beautiful half-Japanese girl, fill the holes in my kimono sleeves with your soft laughter. Lead me to peace. *(Himiko removes a pistol from her kimono sleeve, bows as she offers it to time and space, and places it before her. She kneels and looks again toward her vision of Mieko.)* Mieko, my child. *(Looks in another direction.)* Billy, my beloved husband. *(Looks outward.)* Mother? Can you hear me? Wait for me, Mother. I am coming to have tea with thee. *(Himiko lifts the pistol and aims it toward her throat. Blackout as a gunshot followed by a deafening atomic-like explosion fills the air, leaving behind trails of smoke. Half light up as, from various dark corners, Teruko, Atsuko, Chizuye and Setsuko enter one by one and take staggered positions. As they speak their first words, the women bow in styles reflecting their personalities.)*

SETSUKO. Shall we have tea at three?

TERUKO. Please come over for tea.

ATSUKO. Join me for tea, just the two of us.

CHIZUYE. Tea. O-cha. That's our word for it.

SETSUKO. I drink it hot in a pretty Japanese cup.

TERUKO. I like it cool. Any cup will do.

ATSUKO. Lukewarm in a fancy Japanese cup.

CHIZUYE. Very hot. In a simple cup.

TERUKO. Tea is not quiet.

ATSUKO. But turbulent.

SETSUKO. Tremblings.

CHIZUYE. So fine you can't see them.

SETSUKO. So dense it seems to be standing still.

TERUKO. We Japanese women drink a lot of it.

ATSUKO. Become it.

SETSUKO. Swallow the tempest.

CHIZUYE. And nobody knows.

ATSUKO. The storm inside.

TERUKO. Ever.

SETSUKO. We remain …

TERUKO. Peaceful.

CHIZUYE. Contained.

ATSUKO. The eye of the hurricane.

SETSUKO. But if you can taste the tea.

TERUKO. If it can roll over your tongue in one swallow.

ATSUKO. Then the rest will come to you.

CHIZUYE. When the tea leaves are left behind in the bottom of a cup. *(Himiko reenters carrying Rayban sunglasses and a long, blonde wig.)*

HIMIKO. When we are long gone and forgotten. *(Himiko puts on the sunglasses and holds out her arms in welcome as the other women exit.)*

HIMIKO. Come … it is time for tea. *(Himiko pulls on the wig and crosses along with cross-fading lights to the tatami room.)*

Scene 1

The Art of Tea

Atsuko and Teruko drift to the tatami room where piles of books and a wild-looking blonde wig are on the floor. They take off their shoes outside of the room and enter. Atsuko has brought her own booties and puts them on. She removes her sweater, and studies the room with mixed feelings of revulsion and attraction. Sniffing the air with displeasure, she covers her nose and mouth with a handkerchief. They set up the Japanese-style table and place four zabuton [Japanese sitting cushions] as Himiko observes from the darkness. She is a matter-of-fact spirit on trial, ready to defend herself.

ATSUKO. Ugh. How were you able to have tea here with this stench! *(Studies the floor.)* Maybe we should keep our shoes on.

TERUKO. It didn't smell here before, Atsuko-san!

ATSUKO. Yes, it did. You said it did.

TERUKO. I said it smelled like liquor and burnt candles.

ATSUKO. Well, you know that's from bringing home men and making sex.

TERUKO. *(Insistently protective.)* Before her husband died, Himiko lived a quiet life. *(Atsuko picks up the wig as if to negate Teruko's statement. Teruko starts to exit to the kitchen.)* I'm going to find the teapot and cups. *(Atsuko hurriedly drops the wig and looks around the room as if she suspects ghosts.)*

ATSUKO. Don't leave me alone!

TERUKO. We must begin. *(Exits to kitchen.)*

HIMIKO. Yes, we must begin ... Tea for the soul; tea to cleanse the spirit. *(Atsuko examines the room carefully as if afraid of getting dirty and begins to put things away. She puts on her glasses.)*

ATSUKO. Himiko was so wild after her husband died. Maybe she was like that in Japan, too. I don't know how she passed the screening tests for Army brides. They took so long and the Yankee officers asked so many stupid questions.

HIMIKO. *(Addresses Atsuko as if echoing a reminder, encircling her.)* "Are you a Communist? Why do you want to marry this man instead of one of your own native Japanese? Do you think moving to America will afford you personal financial gain? Are you suffering from insanity? Are you an imbecile or idiot?" *(A pause.)* "Are you now — or have you ever been — a prostitute?"

ATSUKO. The nerve of that American Army! Did the Army ask you if you were a prostitute? *(Teruko returns with a teapot, cups, lacquer coasters and two cloths — one wet and one dry — all on a lacquer tray. She handles them delicately.)*

TERUKO. Yes. I told them we weren't all bad girls just because we fell in love with Americans. Poor Himiko.

ATSUKO. Where is Setsuko Banks? I thought she was the one most friendly with Himiko. *(Looks around the room eerily.)* I heard the tatami was covered with blood. It's funny, isn't it, how one moment someone is full of life and the next, they are ashes.

TERUKO. Atsuko-san, ne, if you're that uncomfortable, go home. Setsuko and Chiz *(Pronounced like "cheese.")* and I can take care of this.

ATSUKO. As head of our Buddhist chapter, how would it look to headquarters if I didn't do everything I could to help a member? *(A vicarious smile as she peers over her glasses.)* Besides, I wanted to see the inside of this house.

TERUKO. Well, Setsuko-san went home to pick up o-sushi.

ATSUKO. And "Chiz" is always late. Her nickname sounds so stupid. Like food. She even wears pants now and grows her hair long like a hippy. *(Removes a crocheted green-and-purple poodle toilet paper cover from the trunk and shakes her head at its oddity.)* She's just as silly as Himiko was. *(Atsuko takes out her own tea cup, admires it, and places it on the table. Teruko wipes Himiko's tea cups, first with a wet cloth and then a dry one. She carefully arranges the cups with coasters and teapot on the table. Atsuko moves Himiko's tea cups away from her own.)*

TERUKO. *(Removes a folded newspaper article from her wallet; reads from it with officiousness.)* Listen. I cut this out. "Death Notices. September 9, 1968. Himiko Hamilton, thirty-nine, widow of Chief Warrant Officer William Hamilton, passed away in her home from a self-inflicted gunshot wound. She was preceded in death by her husband and, recently, her daughter, Mieko, eighteen. A Japanese war bride, Mrs. Hamilton was a resident of Junction City for twenty years. She leaves no survivors."

8

HIMIKO. *(To audience with quiet dignity.)* But, still, I ask you to listen. Please. I am suspended between two worlds. There is no harmony here *(Indicates the women in tatami room.)* nor here. *(Indicates her soul.)*

TERUKO. Well, she *did* leave survivors.

ATSUKO. Who?

TERUKO. Us.

ATSUKO. Not me! Just because I'm Japanese doesn't mean I have anything to do with her life. Dead is dead, Teruko-san, so what difference does it make? Who knows, ne. Maybe next it will be me. Do you think the Japanese women in this town are going to pray for my soul just because I happen to come from Japan?

TERUKO. Atsuko-san. We must respect the dead.

ATSUKO. Only because they no longer have to fear the darkness. The rest of us must wait, without any idea of when our time will come to an end.

TERUKO. *(As if she feels Himiko's presence.)* No, sometimes even the dead must wait. In limbo.

ATSUKO. *(With a smile.)* Well, Himiko should wait forever after what she did to her husband.

TERUKO. But you know what he was doing to her.

ATSUKO. Nobody really knows.

HIMIKO. Nobody would listen.

ATSUKO. Maybe she wasn't a good wife.

HIMIKO. I was the *best* wife.

TERUKO. He never let her out of the house and hardly let her have guests. Remember during the big snow storm? The phone lines were down and —

HIMIKO. — I didn't have any tea or rice left. Billy had gone to Oklahoma to visit his family. He said, "Don't leave the house" and took my daughter, Mieko, with him. So there I was, starving to death, standing behind —

TERUKO. *(Overlapping with Himiko's last two words.)* — Standing behind the frosty glass. She looked like she was made of wax.

HIMIKO. *(Smiles at herself.)* I asked him once. I said, "Why did you marry me?" And he said he wanted a good maid, for free.

ATSUKO. Maybe she wanted too much.

HIMIKO. I never asked for anything. Except soy sauce and good rice. And dreams ... for Mieko. *(Himiko glows with love for her child, turns around and seems to see her as a tot, and beckons to her.)* Mieko-chan! My little girl! *(Himiko exits as if chasing "Mieko.")*

ATSUKO. Teruko, I saw your daughter last week. *(A compliment.)* She looks Japanese. That's nice. Too bad she isn't friends with my girl. My girl's always with Setsuko-san's daughter. Have you seen her? Looks Indonesian, not Japanese at all. Shame, ne.

TERUKO. But Setsuko's daughter is the only one who cooks Japanese food. My daughter likes hamburger sandwich and yellow-haired boys.

ATSUKO. My daughter always goes to Setsuko-san's house. I've never been invited.

TERUKO. Setsuko likes her privacy.

ATSUKO. She invited you to tea.

TERUKO. Well, if you're not willing to be genuine with her, how can you share the honor of tea together?

ATSUKO. She invited Himiko, too!

TERUKO. Yes, even after the incident. Even though everyone was afraid. *(A siren wails as a deafening gunshot echoes and lights black-out. Atsuko and Teruko exit to the kitchen. Himiko, without sunglasses, drifts from the darkness. The siren fades out and a spotlight fades up immediately on Himiko who crouches as if shooting a pistol. Smiling and rising gracefully, she speaks matter-of-factly.)*

HIMIKO. *(Imitates the sound of shots, pronounced "bahn" like in bonfire.)* Ban! Ban! Ban! Yes. I am Himiko Hamilton. The murderess. I married and murdered a gentleman from Oklahoma. And they let me go on self-defense. It took one shot — right through the heart I never knew he had. Now that he's gone, I can speak freely. Please listen. I wasted my life in Kansas. The state — of mind. Not Kansas City, but *Junction City,* a stupid hick town that rests like a pimple on an army base called Fort Riley. Where the Army's resettlement policy exiled our husbands because they were married to "Japs." *(Himiko indicates her own face as Chizuye and Setsuko enter from opposite corners carrying food in a basket and wrapped in furoshiki, respectively.)* They won't tell you that because they're real *Japaneezy* Japanese. *(Chizuye and Setsuko smile and bow formally to each other in greeting; Setsuko bows a second time.)* See what I mean? Well … I'm about as Japanese as corn flakes, or so they say, and I killed my husband because he laughed at my soy sauce just one time too many. *(Himiko smiles whimsically and turns away from the audience. Chizuye and Setsuko drift down stage. They are unaware of Himiko's presence. Setsuko and Chizuye stand outside of the house.)*

SETSUKO. Oh, Chizuye-san, I wish Himiko-san could have seen all the Japanese women at her funeral.

HIMIKO. *(To the audience.)* All the Japanese women who were too ashamed to say hello to me in public because I was "no good."

CHIZUYE. *(Adamant with characteristic exuberance.)* Ever since she shot her husband two years ago, she's kind of haunted me. It made me remember that underneath my comfortable American clothes, I am, after all, Japanese. *(A quick smile.)* But don't tell anybody.

SETSUKO. Well, after all, you were the one who went looking for her.

CHIZUYE. Someone had to. The rest of you were too afraid of what you would find. *(Looks into space as she recalls.)* I forced her door open and, there she was, paler and bluer than the sky over Hiroshima that strange August. She had pulled her kimono over her American dress, as if it might make her journey into the next life a little easier. But I took one look at her and I knew nothing was ever going to be easy for her, not in life or in death.

HIMIKO. I would have given anything to have tea with Japanese girls. *(Setsuko and Chizuye approach the house and remove their shoes. Setsuko straightens hers and Chizuye's.)*

CHIZUYE. What'd you bring?

SETSUKO. Maki-zushi.

CHIZUYE. *(Smiles to poke fun at her friend.)* Figures. I brought spinach quiche, Sue.

SETSUKO. My name is not Sue. My name is Setsuko. Chizuye-san, I tell you many times not to call me by this nickname you made up.

CHIZUYE. But it's easier.

SETSUKO. Like "Chiz." *(Pronounces it "cheese.")*

CHIZUYE. *(Laughs; pronounces it with a short "i.")* No, Setsuko, like "Chiz." That's what my customers at my restaurant call me, but you can call me anything you like. *(They enter the house and Chizuye looks toward the kitchen.)* Hello? Hello? Ah, Teruko! Hello. *(Teruko appears from the kitchen with food, including fruit and maki-zushi. Setsuko scurries to help her.)*

TERUKO. Hello! Hello! Look, Atusko-san is here, too.

CHIZUYE. *(Much surprise and a touch of contempt.)* Atsuko?!

SETSUKO. Well, what an unexpected pleasure.

ATSUKO. Setsuko-san! I rarely see you, but you look younger every time I do. I was sorry to hear about your husband.

SETSUKO. Yes, well, it was his time to … to move on.

ATSUKO. Negroes don't live very long. The food they eat, you know.

11

SETSUKO. My husband ate almost entirely Japanese food.

TERUKO. Atsuko-san's husband hates Japanese food. *(Giggles.)* And he's Japanese American!

ATSUKO. He does *not* hate Japanese food! *(To Setsuko and Chiz.)* Why are you both so late? We cleaned the kitchen already. And, of course, we must have tea.

SETSUKO. Oh, yes, tea sounds very good to me now.

TERUKO. Why, yes. Everything must start with tea.

CHIZUYE. *(Laughs.)* Tea is *just* a drink.

SETSUKO. Oh, it's much more than that.

ATSUKO. I couldn't live without tea.

HIMIKO. Yes … it brings everything into balance.

ATSUKO. I think it improves my eyesight.

SETSUKO. *(Laughing.)* And my insight. *(Teruko, Setsuko and Atsuko have a good laugh over this as Chizuye looks on dead-pan. Finally, she smiles and lights a cigarette.)*

CHIZUYE. Hey, enough about tea. Who else is coming?

TERUKO. More than four would be too many. I stopped asking for volunteers after Atsuko-san spoke up.

CHIZUYE. How many were there?

TERUKO. At least fifty Japanese women!

CHIZUYE. Fifty? Jesus. You'd think it was a blue-light special.

SETSUKO. Chizuye-san! Shame, ne! After all, this is a difficult occasion for us the first time a member of our Japanese community has passed on.

CHIZUYE. What "community"?

HIMIKO. *(Again, to audience.)* Yes, what community? We knew each other, but not really … We didn't care enough to know.

CHIZUYE. Who's got time to chit-chat, right, "Ats"? *(Pronounced with a short "a," like "ahts.")* Now that I'm finally having tea with the great Atsuko Yamamoto, you get a nickname.

ATSUKO. Thank you, but you can keep your … gift. It's obvious we're all from different neighborhoods.

SETSUKO. But we are all Army wives — and we are all Japanese.

CHIZUYE. So what? That won't buy us a ticket to Nirvana. Let's face it, girls, after we get through dealing with our jobs and our families, we're ready to go to sleep. And, if any of us are willing to drive across town and have tea, we don't even talk about what's really on our minds — whether coming to America was such a good idea. *(A bitter smile.)* Countries last; love is mortal.

SETSUKO. But we're here today because we're Japanese.

CHIZUYE. We're here today because we're scared.

HIMIKO. Scared they will be next to die or their souls will be left in limbo like mine.

ATSUKO. *(Hardly able to contain her excitement at being able to ask a question she has pondered for years:)* Tell us, Setsuko-san. Is it true about Himiko being a dance hall girl in Japan?

SETSUKO. If that's what she said. I never really knew her until after her husband died. I would see her walking in the middle of a humid summer day in a heavy coat and the yellow-haired wig.

HIMIKO. *(Re-living that day.)* "Hello. I am Mrs. William Hamilton. May I have a glass of water? Oh, thank you, thank you. You are so kind."

ATSUKO. *(Gesticulating that Himiko was crazy.)* Kichigai, ne ...

CHIZUYE. She was *not* crazy.

TERUKO. It is the Japanese way to carry everything inside.

HIMIKO. Yes. And that is where I hid myself.

ATSUKO. She came from Japan, but the way she dressed, the way she walked. Mah, I remember the district church meeting. She came in a low-cut dress and that yellow-haired wig, *(Mocks how she thinks a Korean walks.)* walking like a Korean.

CHIZUYE. Cut it out, Ats.

SETSUKO. So ne, we have something in common with all the Oriental women here, even the Vietnamese. We all left behind our countries to come and live here with the men we loved.

ATSUKO. Okay, okay. It's not that I didn't like Himiko-san. So many things she did were not acceptable. If she acted like that in Japan, people would think she was ... well, a prostitute. Something was not right inside her head. I mean, whoever heard of a Japanese shooting her husband with a rifle? I told you that day at the cemetery. *(Himiko, having had enough, rushes forward and the women freeze.)*

HIMIKO. *(Defiantly calls them back into the past with a roll call, stamping her foot as she calls out each name.)* Teruko. Setsuko. Atsuko. Chizuye. *(Himiko exits as the music for "Taps" begins. The women drift from the house as if answering roll call. The lights fade out on house and fade up down stage. They stand as if around a head-stone at a cemetery as Himiko enters. A black-veiled hat, black coat and black pumps complete her widow ensemble. She carries a black bag out of which she pulls a can of beer. The women watch in shock as Himiko opens the beer and pours it over the "grave" by which they stand. Setsuko runs to her and takes the beer.)* Mah, there must be a thousand graves here!

13

SETSUKO. Shame on you, Himiko-san! Pouring beer on your husband's grave!

HIMIKO. I am celebrating. First Memorial Day since he "left me." He liked beer when he was alive. Why shouldn't he like it when he's dead?

CHIZUYE. Sounds pretty fair to me.

ATSUKO. Teruko-san, come. We've seen enough. *(Atsuko pulls away a reluctant Teruko who beckons to Chiz. All three exit. Setsuko, concerned, lingers as Himiko suddenly looks up at an invisible object in great shock.)*

HIMIKO. I'm sorry, Billy. That's right. I forgot. You like Budweiser beer. This is cheap kind, brand X. See? Just B-E-E-R. Billy, what are you doing here? I believe in reincarnation, but this is a little soon. I planned on being gone before you came back. I'm sorry I didn't bury you in your favorite shirt. I couldn't fix the hole in it from when I shot you. No, no. I don't want to go with you. *(Struggling with him.)* No, I want to stay here with our daughter. She's not mad at me for what I did. She says you deserved it. No, I don't want to be alone with you anymore. I don't want to kiss and make up. *(Pushes away the unseen presence.)* Setchan! Help me! Billy's going to take me away. *(The presence knocks her off her feet.)*

SETSUKO. *(An antithetical picture of solitude, she draws near.)* Himiko-san. Let's go home now. We'll make tea and talk.

HIMIKO. Help me, Setchan. He's going to beat me up again.

SETSUKO. Come, Himi-chan. You must go home and rest.

HIMIKO. There is only unrest. It is like the war never ended.

SETSUKO. *(Sympathetically.)* Oh, Himi-san. *(Not knowing what else to do, she releases Himiko and bows her head sorrowfully.)*

HIMIKO. *(Enervated, to herself.)* I wish I would have died in World War Two. It was an easier war than this one. *(Himiko exits offstage as Setsuko removes her shoes and returns to the tatami room and lights cross-fade into Scene Two …)*

Scene 2

Selecting Tea

Lights up on the house where Atsuko stands wearing an apron over her clothing. Teruko sits at the table arranging three tins of tea, a porcelain tea pot, and the tea cups. Setsuko sorts through the trunk, removing such things as a photo album, materials, and green and purple crocheted poodle toilet paper covers. A tea kettle whistles loudly from the offstage kitchen. The noise jars everybody.

ATSUKO. *(To the offstage Chiz.)* Chizuye-san. What kind of tea would you like?

CHIZUYE. I'm looking for coffee. Isn't there any coffee around here?

TERUKO. *(Gets up, prepared to go.)* I'll go to the store and buy some for her.

ATSUKO. Why do we need to waste time with that? There's tea.

SETSUKO. She just wants coffee. She's tired.

ATSUKO. She just wants to have coffee because we're having tea. She even brought egg pie. Ugh.

TERUKO. I like egg pie. *(On a look from Atsuko.)* Sometimes.

CHIZUYE. *(Enters holding up a jar triumphantly.)* Instant coffee! What will we Americans think of next?

ATSUKO. Did you learn that at English class?

CHIZUYE. Why? You want to go to class with me, Ats?

TERUKO. *(Interested.)* What do you learn there?

CHIZUYE. English. *(A pause; smiling.)* You should learn English.

ATSUKO. She knows English!

CHIZUYE. I mean real English. *(To Teruko.)* Ever seen *My Fair Lady*? *(Teruko's face is blank.)* You know Audrey Hepburn?

TERUKO. Yes! Yes! *Breakfast at Tiffany!* *(A pause; excitedly but with surprise.)* She goes to English class, too?

CHIZUYE. No, no, no. But in *My Fair Lady*, she starts out like you and ends up like me. *(Chizuye laughs, something Atsuko does not appreciate. Atsuko gets back to the matter at hand by tapping a spoon on the side of a tea cup.)*

ATSUKO. We have plain green tea, roasted rice tea, and just a little premium green tea.

TERUKO. Plain tea, please.

ATSUKO. Plain tea?

CHIZUYE. It's peasant tea, Teruko.

TERUKO. I like it.

ATSUKO. You have such simple tastes.

TERUKO. Makes life easier, yo.

SETSUKO. Well, roasted rice tea is fine.

ATSUKO. I like premium.

CHIZUYE. Of course.

SETSUKO. We'll let Atsuko choose. *(Teruko starts to open the premium tin, but Atsuko pulls out a pretty tea tin from her bag and smiles like a reigning queen.)*

ATSUKO. I brought my own! Shall I treat you? *(Everybody but Chizuye nods.)*

CHIZUYE. Once in a while I still drink green tea, but I choose my drink like I chose my husband: strong, dark and with a lot of sugar.

ATSUKO. *(Extremely offended.)* Really, Chizuye-san!

CHIZUYE. Aw, loosen up, Ats!

ATSUKO. *(Repulsed.)* Did you husband teach you to talk like that?

CHIZUYE. *(Ready to take her to the mat.)* You don't know anything about my husband.

TERUKO. *(Leaps into the conflict to avoid confrontation, hands each woman a plate of food.)* Well … what do you think our husbands thought about us when they met us? *(The other women look at Teruko with accustomed strangeness. Chizuye is not quite ready to relinquish her fight, but does so out of respect for Teruko and Setsuko.)* I mean, there they were, in a strange land full of people they had never seen before. We were eighteen or nineteen, didn't speak too much English. Why do you really think they wanted to marry us?

SETSUKO. For the same reason we wanted to marry them. We were young and we fell in love. So many of us.

CHIZUYE. I don't think there were that many.

SETSUKO. Oh yes. My daughter read that over a hundred thousand of us married Americans after World War Two.

CHIZUYE. That many?

TERUKO. *(With her customary amusing innocence.)* That's a lot of love! *(As the lights fade out on the house, Himiko, without sunglasses, enters and comes down stage center. She wears a pretty, youthful kimono. A light fades up on her and a period song such as "Don't Sit*

Under the Apple Tree with Anyone Else but Me" fades in to mark the post-war era in Japan. * The other women drift down stage and occupy various background positions of the stage as they don pretty kimono as well.)

HIMIKO. War's over. Strange-looking tall men with big noses and loud mouths are running our country. Our new supreme commander is called MacArthur, the great military savior who will preserve our ravaged nation ... but who cannot preserve the common soul. *(A pause.)* Last night, coming home from a wedding, I see my mother in her best kimono walking by the river. She takes off her geta and puts her feet in the water. Her face is peaceful. So lovely, like the moon in the shadows of the clouds. She slips her small hand into the river and picks up a large stone. Looking at it for only a moment, she drops it in her kimono sleeve. Suddenly, she begins filling both sleeves with stones. I try to stop her, but she fights. The same stones I played with as a child sagging in her kimono sleeves, she jumps into the currents. I watch her sink, her long black hair swirling around her neck like a silk noose. Her white face, a fragile lily; the river, a typhoon. I wondered what it felt like to be a flower in a storm. *("The Wedding March" begins and the women move as if in an American ceremony toward center stage, all formally except for Himiko. All come down stage center looking outward, their expressions a varied repertoire. Setsuko smiles confidently. Teruko is meek, but decided. Himiko is arrogant. Atsuko smiles uncertainly. Chizuye stands and joins them. The music rises to an uncomfortable pitch and ceases. Though facing the audience, the women share experiences happily as if stripped of inhibitions. Their demeanor and carriage reflect their youth.)*

TERUKO. *(A pert, cute bow.)* I come from Fukuoka.

SETSUKO. *(An elegant, formal bow.)* Me, from the great port city of Kobe.

CHIZUYE. *(A quick, crisp bow.)* Yokohama.

ATSUKO. *(An official bow.)* Nagoya.

HIMIKO. And me from the capital of the magnificent Empire of Japan: Tokyo. *(She bows exuberantly, flipping her hair back. Lights widen as the women relax and take staggered positions. The lights focus from one to the next.)*

TERUKO. We live in a small house next to my father's lumber business. I'm hanging clothes to dry as the white Yankee walks by.

---

* See Special Note on Songs and Recordings on copyright page.

He says, "Why, hello, sugar pie! *(Pronounced "shuga pie.")* Ain't you the purtiest thing!" I say no. He says yes. I say okay.

SETSUKO. And Father says, "Don't look at them! They'll rape you." He even confided to me they had tails. But on the way home from dressmaking school, the Yankee soldier's helmet falls off at my feet. What can I do? I give it back to him. For the first time, I look into the gentle eyes of a man the color of — soy sauce!

ATSUKO. *(Removes a fan from her kimono sleeve and uses it girlishly.)* Coming home from countryside to visit my aunt, I stop at market. Suddenly … there he is! A Japanese man in American uniform from California. He speaks bad Japanese. Sounds cute! He wants to give me a ride. *(Sharply slaps the fan closed against her leg.)* But I can hear my mother *(Speaks as if she's become her mother, an adamant and proud Japanese.)* "Japanese Americans not Japanese anymore! They speak loud and marry foreigners. They don't even take a bath every night." *(Again, the fan opens and moves girlishly.)* He looked clean! But I say to soldier, "Sorry. No thank you, sir." *(Bragging with joy.)* He followed me all the way to the train station!

HIMIKO. It's tough in Tokyo after the Yankees take our country. I have six sisters. My father screams about all the daughters my mother left him with. "Too crowded, no money." If I want a new dress, I have to work for it. There is this cabaret. My girlfriend says let's go be dancers. I think she means onstage. Like movies, dancing in pretty dresses while people watch and clap. I find out too late it means dancing with Americans. Fifty yen-a-dance.

CHIZUYE. My mother died when I was born so it's always just Father and me. His best friend runs a restaurant that's pretty popular after the war with all the American boys. The first time I see Gustavo is there. Father and his friend — and his friend's marriage-hungry son — have me surrounded on all sides. But what they don't have covered is my heart. *(All exit except for Teruko and Chizuye. Music — perhaps "Tokyo Boogie Woogie" — sets the post-war mood in Japan again.* * *Chizuye immediately assumes the persona of an older, intrusive matchmaker. She stands behind the effervescent Teruko as if sneaking up on her.)*

TERUKO. 1947. The business is picking up. We hold the yearly national barber competition and I win! First woman to win! Since the day he walked by my house, Master Sergeant Curtis Mackenzie comes to our barber shop again and again. He comes too much!

* See Special Note on Songs and Recordings on copyright page.

Soon he will have no hair left!

CHIZUYE. Excuse me.

TERUKO. Yes.

CHIZUYE. That American. That nice-looking Texas man over there? He wants to take you to a movie. He's very nice. I cut his hair every week.

TERUKO. Explain to him.

CHIZUYE. Come on, Teru-chan, give him a chance. One little date. I won't tell anybody.

TERUKO. Tell him I can't be seen with a Yankee.

CHIZUYE. He said he will take you and a girlfriend to a movie. In fact, he said he will take everyone at the barber shop to a movie.

TERUKO. What? The four of us plus the three girls in back?

CHIZUYE. Yes. If that's what it takes to get a date with you. *(Chizuye disappears in the darkness.)*

TERUKO. We walk on opposite sides of the street. Seven women on one side; you on the other. At the movie house, as if by chance, we sit next to each other. For a year, we go just like that, every week. Maybe fifty movies. Seven women. You spend a lot of yen, ne, just to get to know this silly country girl. *(Blackout on Teruko; simultaneous spotlight goes up on Himiko who dances romantically to a slow American 1940s rhythm and blues song.)*

HIMIKO. It was simple; it was a job. "Good evening. Welcome, welcome. Fifty yen. Do you want a dance, soldier?" *(Mimics taking money and stands in surprise.)* Five hundred yen! No, no. Too much. Take it back, please. *(Offers it back.)*

CHIZUYE. *(Immediately appears and stands close to Himiko; the persona of the matchmaker continues, but in the style of a dyke-ish, dance hall madam.)* Girl-san. That Yankee soldier over there. He wants to take you to dinner.

HIMIKO. I don't leave with customers.

CHIZUYE. Ah, but one date won't hurt, will it, Himiko-san? No one has to know. *(Touches Himiko sexually, who is taken aback by this.)* After all, like he says, this is a dance hall.

HIMIKO. Yes. That is exactly what we do and all that we do — dance.

CHIZUYE. You'll never get anywhere thinking like that. *(Chizuye disappears in the darkness.)*

HIMIKO. His name was Billy, a cute white boy from Oklahoma. He came back every week and danced only with me. Never said too much, but he brought me flowers every time. He taught me how to do the "lindy hop" *(She begins dancing and twirls around, finally stopping full of laughter; it settles into a smile.)* … among other things. *(A pause.)* It was my first time. *(A pause.)* There was a teacher. Japanese. He taught at a university at Aoyama. He liked me. Truly. I was going to marry him. Good family. But I can't tell him I wasn't working at the trading company as an operator anymore. I can't tell him I am no longer respectable. So I just say I am sorry. I say my family won't accept the marriage. And I go back to the cabaret and wait for Billy. *(Blackout on Himiko; spotlight on Atsuko and Setsuko, unaware of each others' presence. They come forward.)*

ATSUKO. We are shopping at the market.

SETSUKO. We are waiting for a train.

ATSUKO. Mr. Kazuhiro Yamamoto, the Californian, is buying fish. So cute his face. He says, "Buy. Fish. This one. *(Indicates fish.)* "Kore," and looks at me for help with his Japanese — as the shopkeeper laughs and overcharges him! I say it's wrong to cheat him and protect my *Japanese* American fiancé.

SETSUKO. It begins to rain. Will the color of his skin wash off? I watch his wrist and wait, but *(To her pleasure.)* it stays brown. He is a "military policeman" with great power. But he has gentle eyes; I don't know how he could have killed in the war. *(A pause.)* Most of my girlfriends who married Americans are long gone. Creed goes, too, but we write — my bad English and his bad Japanese. He gets stationed in Tokyo after Korean war and, for five years, we date while I care for my Mother. One August, I hold her and she dies in my arms. My bond with Japan gone, I can now leave. *(A pause as she smiles.)* Creed and I marry. He says it's not like Dick and Jane getting hitched in Peoria! *(The women address the unseen presences of their husbands.)*

TERUKO. You are so white, like a ghost, ne. How can I be sure you will never look at another woman? I hear you have many yellow-haired girls in America. How can I be sure my black hair and different eyes will still be what you want?

SETSUKO. You say we may live the Japanese way wherever we go. I can't give up being Japanese even in your America. This war drove my father to take his life. I gave up enough. I want peace.

ATSUKO. Well, you look Japanese. It isn't like marrying a real Yankee. Well, it isn't!

CHIZUYE. You keep telling me you're Mexican and that life isn't always easy in America. I'm not sure what that means, but you have taught me this word "love" and I think that's what I feel for you.

Life is short, Gustavo, and I have never felt like such a woman before. Take me with you. Hurry, before I see the tears in my father's eyes.

HIMIKO. My father doesn't want me to show my face at home again. "Look at your big belly," he shouts, "carrying Yankee-gai-jin baby. Shame. Shame." Billy, you have to take me to America now. There's no life left for me in Japan. People whisper "whore" in the streets and spit at my feet. You brought the war into my heart. *(A pause, as if getting married.)* Yes. I do. Until death do us part.

TERUKO. They are taller.

SETSUKO. And kinder.

ATSUKO. And cleaner.

HIMIKO. And richer.

CHIZUYE. Our men have lost their spirit.

TERUKO. It is hard after the war.

SETSUKO. We will soon be twenty.

ATSUKO. Soon too old for marriage.

HIMIKO. I am tired of living in the Tokyo the Yankees left us with. *(They look outward and begin removing their kimono to reveal their original outfits underneath. They put the kimono away.)*

CHIZUYE. Father, forgive me. I should be here to take care of you when you're old.

TERUKO. Mother, please, stop crying. I'm not crazy. I love him.

SETSUKO. Dear mother, thank you for your blessing of Creed and me.

ATSUKO. My parents stop talking to me. I can't help it. He's the one I want to spend my life with. Forgive me. *(Bows low.)*

HIMIKO. Good-bye Father ... *(Regret and sadness.)* ... sisters. You shall never see me again.

CHIZUYE. Father weeps like a grandmother. "Write me, Chizu-chan!" he cries. "If you don't like it there, let me know and I'll come and get you myself." "Sayonara," he says, addressing me like a son. And I depart, my heart divided between two men like a dark, shameful canyon.

SETSUKO. We are a casualty the Japanese do not care to count.

CHIZUYE. Excess baggage America does not want to carry.

TERUKO. And so the country watches as thousands of us leave Japan behind.

ATSUKO. And it aches. And it cries.

CHIZUYE. And it hopes we will not be lucky.

SETSUKO. Or brave.

TERUKO. Or accepted.

ATSUKO. Or rich.

HIMIKO. But between the hate they have for us.

CHIZUYE. The disdain.

SETSUKO. The contempt.

TERUKO. There is a private envy.

ATSUKO. Silent jealousy.

HIMIKO. Longing.

CHIZUYE. Yes.

SETSUKO. They want to wear our shoes.

TERUKO. Leave Japan and their war-ragged lives behind.

ATSUKO. Because the mess finally seems too much to clean.

HIMIKO. And Japan finally looks as small as it really is.

CHIZUYE. The war makes them see Japan is not the strongest or best.

SETSUKO. It makes us see — just once — beyond our tiny country and our tiny minds.

TERUKO. *(Salutes, mocking an American Army officer in a booming voice.)* "Attention!"

ATSUKO. "All wives of American military personnel must wear pants on board ship during the entire fifteen-day journey."

HIMIKO. "Attention, all wives of American military personnel, socks and shoes must be worn at all times."

CHIZUYE. "I repeat socks *and* shoes."

SETSUKO. "Husbands and wives will be confined to separate sleeping quarters."

TERUKO. "That's all."

HIMIKO. *(As herself, quietly.)* For now. *(A single spotlight of interrogation grows tight; the women are drawn to it as if by mandate. All crowd together and stand at attention. Himiko is less serious than the others. Teruko, unsure, follows Atsuko's movement and attitude. The women clear their throats. As they speak, they exchange looks which indicate unsure commitment to or a lack of understanding for the words. Setsuko and Atsuko raise their right hands. Teruko raises her left and then changes to her right, following Atsuko's example. Atsuko glances at Himiko who, with great boredom, raises her right hand. Only Chizuye is confident; she says the words well and with command.)*

WOMEN. *(In unison; with difficulty, stumbling over various words as this is the first time they have seen or read these words; some can say almost none of the words.)* "I hereby declare, on oath, that I absolutely renounce all allegiance to any foreign state or sovereignty of which I have heretofore been a citizen; that I will defend laws of United States of America against all enemies; that I will bear arms on behalf of United States; and that I take this obligation freely without any mental reservation. So help me God."

CHIZUYE. *(With pride and a sense of great accomplishment.)* That's it.

ATSUKO. What? Did anybody understand any of that?

SETSUKO. Defend against all enemies? Aren't we enemy?

HIMIKO. Yes. Bear arms?

TERUKO. *(Nodding at Atsuko for confirmation.)* Freely?

CHIZUYE. Without *any* mental reservation!

SETSUKO. So help me …

ATSUKO. God? *(Chizuye sings "My Country 'Tis of Thee" and enjoins the others to sing along. Teruko is willing and joins in. They hold hands and smile and sing with joy. Setsuko softly sings the Japanese national anthem, "Kimi Ga Yo." Atsuko, after studying Chizuye's choice for a brief moment, joins Setsuko and sings. But, as Himiko begins singing "My Country 'Tis of Thee" in a jarring, life-or-death manner, the women all grow quiet and sing the final lyrics with her, but with altered words. They sing with a sense of fear.)*

WOMEN. "Land where our souls will die. Land of our children's pride. From every mountainside, let freedom ring." *(Lights cross-fade to Scene Three as Chizuye, Teruko, Atsuko and Setsuko return to the tatami and lights fade up. Himiko moves to side stage and observes:)*

Scene 3

Serving Tea

Atsuko pours tea as the others begin to examine the trunk's contents.

CHIZUYE. *(Holds up her coffee cup.)* Here's to fairy tales — and the dust they become.

HIMIKO. *(To audience, insistently.)* No, no, they must drink for hope. *(Setsuko, Teruko and Atsuko lift their tea cups and sip. Teruko reacts as if she burned her tongue.)*

TERUKO. A-cha-cha-cha-cha!

ATSUKO. Don't drink so fast, ne. Burn your mouth. *(Tastes it.)* It's not hot at all.

HIMIKO. It's hard to find the perfect temperature.

SETSUKO. It's fine. I like it this way, too.

CHIZUYE. Funny. You two like your tea the same way, your daughters are best friends, your husbands used to go hunting together — and you two probably haven't said a dozen words to each other over the last fifteen years. Is this the first time you've ever had tea together?

HIMIKO. It is, isn't it, Setsuko-san?

SETSUKO. I'm busy with my family. And I have so much sewing to do.

HIMIKO. What is your excuse, Atsuko-san?

ATSUKO. I keep busy with the church.

HIMIKO. And Teruko?

TERUKO. I try to visit everyone, but I like to play Bingo with my sugar pie. And, you know, three times a year we go to Las Vegas.

CHIZUYE. I don't have time either. After Gustavo left the Army, we spent all our time together. Then ... he was gone and, well, I started classes.

HIMIKO. Everybody has an alibi for silence.

CHIZUYE. *(Smiles at the women to tease them.)* Besides, no one ever invited me to take tea but Setsuko.

ATSUKO. I thought you didn't like tea.

CHIZUYE. Don't hand me that bull, Ats. You know you didn't want me in your house because my husband was Mexican. *(Slowly without hostility as she moves from woman to woman.)* Atsuko believes she's the only pure soul left. But, Ats, I have to tell you ... you have no soul. *(Atsuko, taken aback, gets up and moves away. Chizuye stands and walks toward her.)* Don't worry — I don't either.

TERUKO. Chizuye-san!

CHIZUYE. And, Teruko, you think your white husband buys you a position in town society, but, deep down at heart, you're still a "Jap" to them and you always will be. *(Setsuko looks away.)* Setsuko, you live like a social worker. You've had to deal with so much prejudice you don't want *any*body else to feel pain.

SETSUKO. I enjoy taking tea. With any of you.

TERUKO. My husband doesn't like when we speak Japanese. He says it sounds like silverware dropping. So it's better if I take tea at someone else's home.

ATSUKO. Well, I'm not ashamed to say it: I only take tea with my very best friends.

CHIZUYE. Which is to say you don't take it very often.

ATSUKO. *(Boldly faces Chizuye, who does not back off.)* Chizuye, there's no reason to spite me because my husband is Japanese American.

CHIZUYE. Do you think I have any respect for Japanese Americans?

ATSUKO. *(Quickly, adamant.)* They're our people. My husband's parents died in a concentration camp in the California desert, just because they were Japanese.

CHIZUYE. They're not "our" people. They hate us more than Americans because we remind them of what they don't want to be anymore. They made a choice; most of us haven't. They don't like you either, Ats, because you're a "war bride."

ATSUKO. *(Indignant.)* I'm not a war bride. I didn't marry the war.

SETSUKO. Maybe we did.

CHIZUYE. And then we came here — to Kansas. Not quite the fairy tale ending you ordered, eh, Ats? *(As Chizuye laughs gruffly and darkly, the truth of this statement jars them. Clouded with discomfort, they lift their tea cups and drink, except for Chizuye who stares off into the distance. Lights fade out on the tatami area. down stage center, a spotlight fades up on Himiko. She wears her black sunglasses. A typically 1950s Kansas song — perhaps "How Much is That Doggie in the Window" — fades in as Himiko pirouettes and then speaks in the manner of a carnival barker.* In the background in dim light, the others kneel as if just having arrived in Kansas. When Himiko addresses them, they smile, unaware that they are the joke.)*

HIMIKO. "Welcome, welcome, to the Land of Milk and Honey, the Bible Belt; the land of great, wide plains and *(With pride.)* narrow minds. On behalf of the tourism bureau, we'd like to welcome you to Kansas, the Sunflower State. We know all about you people. We read the magazines. We saw the cartoons. We saw *Sayonara.*" *(Himiko bows ridiculously and the women respond sincerely with bows; Himiko returns to her own persona.)* It was more than racism. It was the gloating of victor over enemy. It was curiosity about our yellow skin, about why in the hell their red-blooded American boys would want to bring home an "Oriental." *(She indicates the other women.)* Some of them liked us; most of them didn't. *(Exits; the music fades out, and the others move down stage.)*

ATSUKO. Tell me, miss, do you have a Japanese restaurant here?

* See Special Note on Songs and Recordings on copyright page.

I want to surprise my husband. No Japanese restaurant? Ara! What kind of restaurant do you have? Steak? Barbecue? *(Pronounced bah-bee-q.)* What is barbecue?

SETSUKO. Excuse me. We are looking for a hotel. Interracial couple? What does that mean? You reserve the right to refuse service? But what did we do wrong? My husband works for your government. We just need a place to stay for the night. I *am* speaking English!

TERUKO. *(Fearfully.)* Please stop staring at me like I am an animal. I just want to buy groceries. *(Less fearfully.)* What? You want to be my friend? Oh, how ... how nice! *(Mimics shaking the person's hand, something she find strange; bows at the same time and then, uncomfortable, draws her hand back without malice.)* You have such beautiful yellow hair! Like the color of Japanese pickles!

CHIZUYE. *(Determinedly and to the point.)* Listen, lady, you give me a hard time about opening a checking account just because I'm Japanese, and I'll give you more hell than you bargained for. *I'm an American citizen now. (But she slightly mispronounces the word "citizen.")*

TERUKO. I miss sashimi!

CHIZUYE. It would be nice to bite into o-manju.

SETSUKO. I can taste the crisp nashi.

ATSUKO. Sasa-dango.

TERUKO. Kushi-dango.

CHIZUYE. Hot oden.

SETSUKO. Kaki. There's nothing like Japanese persimmons.

ATSUKO. He never told me there would be no Japanese food.

SETSUKO. He never told me about "we reserve the right."

CHIZUYE. I never thought he would die and leave me here to be an American without him.

TERUKO. I never thought they would be scared of us, too. *(The shrill whistle of a tea kettle blasts through the air, bringing the women back to the tatami room. Himiko enters and drifts. Periodically, she rests and rubs her feet as if they are sore.)*

TERUKO. More tea.

HIMIKO. *(To audience.)* Yes. Please. They *must* keep drinking.

ATSUKO. You didn't mix up the tea cups, did you? *(The women react to Atsuko's idiosyncrasy.)*

TERUKO. I think this one is mine.

SETSUKO. This one is mine. *(Teruko serves fresh tea to everyone and Teruko freshens Chizuye's coffee.)*

26

CHIZUYE. Now, Ats, take it easy.

ATSUKO. She talks just like the women at the grocery store.

TERUKO. Yes, but she gets through the checkout line faster than any of us, too.

SETSUKO. She's always adapted faster than us.

ATSUKO. So, ne, I could never even get used to American bed. In Japan, I always sleep right on the edge of the blankets so my nose could smell the sweet straw of the matting. I come to America and every night for months I fall out of bed!

SETSUKO. One day — I am so embarrassed — Creed sees me in the bathroom. He says, "Setsuko! You're standing on the toilet! Sit down." So I sit — facing the wall. Next time, he laughs and says, "Honey, you're sitting on it backwards. Turn around."

TERUKO. You know this car wash on Sixth Street? I want to surprise my sugar pie by washing the car for him. So I drive through about twenty-five miles an hour! The machines scrape the car. When I come out of there, there are bumps all over and I tell that manager he better pay me for the damage. He just laughs and calls my husband.

SETSUKO. *(Looks at the placid Chizuye.)* Was it always so easy for you?

CHIZUYE. Well, I live *here.* I make the best of it.

SETSUKO. Japan. America. Maybe it doesn't matter where we go. Back home, country papa-san says to me when my first is born, "Bring *it* here for me to see." He wants to see how ugly she is. But she is pretty, and the Japanese crowd and stare. She doesn't look Japanese, they say, and she doesn't look Negro. And I am glad because I have created something new, something that will look new and think new.

CHIZUYE. *(A chuckle which she knows will irritate Atsuko.)* Hybrid Japanese.

TERUKO. Mixed Japanese kids at school are very smart. Teachers say they've never seen anything like it.

ATSUKO. That's only because they're half Japanese.

CHIZUYE. Ats, may your daughter marry a Mexican. *(At this remark, Atsuko almost chokes on her tea.)*

TERUKO. Japanese-Mexican girls are pretty.

ATSUKO. I don't expect Chizuye to understand the importance of being Japanese.

CHIZUYE. Oh, Teri's *(Notes Teruko.)* all right because her daughter came out looking Japanese. Buddha was good to her for chanting all these years. *(Rubs her hands together to make fun of chanting.)*

ATSUKO.   At least none of our girls turned out like Mieko Hamilton.

HIMIKO.   But they are like Mieko. They're between two worlds. We put them there.

ATSUKO.   Mieko was just like her mother.

HIMIKO.   Yes. And like her father.

ATSUKO.   Himiko was crazy and she drove her husband crazy.

CHIZUYE.   And I think you're crazy, so it's all relative, Ats.

TERUKO.   It's nice to be together again, ne. *(Lights cross-fade from tatami to down stage center as women march quietly in military formation to a period military song and drumbeat. Himiko comes center stage.)*

HIMIKO.   Our husbands didn't know what they were getting into. They brought us to Kansas, their Japanese wives dressed up in American clothes. We were little, breakable dolls to them. I don't think they ever really understood us, but they loved us. Even when the memories of the war crashed through their heads like an endless nightmare, they tried hard to keep on living like normal people and to be the husbands they had dreamed about being when they laid their lives on the line for their country. *(As the women file into place and stand at attention, Himiko joins them. They appear rigid, stoic with the carriage of men. Setsuko breaks line and takes on the persona of a tender, Southern gentleman Negro.)*

SETSUKO.   Uh, Baby-san, why are you staring at the washing machine? The clothes should have been done an hour ago. Yes, I said you don't have to do a thing. Yes, I promised it's all automatic. But, honey, even when it's automatic, you have to push the button to turn it on. *(Setsuko falls back into formation. Atsuko takes on the persona of a mellow, California nisei and steps forward.)*

ATSUKO.   Hey, Atsuko, where'd you put my hammer? I gotta finish these shelves and I know you never put it back when you use it. Now don't get upset. I'm not trying to say you don't ever do anything right. I just want my hammer. Are you on the rag or what? *(The imaginary hammer comes flying through the air and he barely catches it.)* Okay, okay. Sorry. I didn't mean it. Aw, honey, please don't make me sleep on the couch. *(The hammer hits its mark. Atsuko falls back into line. Chizuye falls out.)*

CHIZUYE.   Hey, Chizuye. I'm happy you've learned to cook Mexican food, but can you cook some Japanese food for me? The enchilada is fine, but I love Japanese food. What do you say you teach me how to make yaki-soba? *(Chizuye falls back into line. Teruko breaks line and takes on the persona of a robust, swaggering Texan.)*

TERUKO. You did *what* to the car at the car wash? Hell, Teri, ain't you got any sense in that little Japanese head of yours? You don't drive *through* the car wash. You just sit in the damn car and let the machines roll the car. I'll be damned, my new car lit'rally gone down the drain. *(Reacts to a crying Teruko, softens.)* Now, honey, don't cry. We'll just have to get the car fixed. *(Falls back into formation.)* Again.

HIMIKO. *(Falls out of formation with the persona of a scrappy Oklahoman with an edgy, rural voice.)* Himi, I didn't stay out late. I told you. I was fishing with Kaz Yamamoto. Okay, okay, so I fished all night and only brought home two fish. What can I say? I'm a bad fisherman. You want to go out for ice cream? There's a Peter Pan store right up the street. I'll get you some Oregon blackberry. I'll bet you never had that flavor before. What? Wait a minute, these ain't frozen fillets from the grocery store. Shut up before I knock your friggin' teeth in, you hear me, Himi? *(Himiko falls back into formation. The "men" break line and ad lib hearty greetings. Two go through the motions of cleaning and loading rifles; two open the beers and mimic drinking. Campsite activity ensues.)*

TERUKO. Yo, beer.

ATSUKO. Yeah.

HIMIKO. Ain't nothing' like a huntin' trip to clear out the lungs, ain't it, boys?

TERUKO. Kinda like shooting at Japs again. Ooooooops. I didn't mean it that way. Y'all know how it was during the war, "do this to the Japs," "do that to the Japs." Sorry. Slip of the tongue. 'Course mine always has been kinda swinging' on a loose hinge. *(As he pats Atsuko on the shoulder.)* I mean, you know I got a good heart. *(He turns and mimics shooting a basket.)* Two points.

ATSUKO. *(Takes his turn at shooting, makes the basket and ad libs victory.)* My friends said I married one of my own kind. Uh-uh. I spent my life trying to be American, not Japanese American. Being American was better. *(Atsuko and Setsuko exchange a handshake of fraternity.)*

SETSUKO. Left the genteel South and grew up hard in New York. I had ladies throwing a lot of fast words and a lot of fast action in my face for years. When I met Setsuko, I knew I could live the quiet life I love, and she'd be right there with me. Forever.

TERUKO. Before World War Two, I never dated anything but white tomatoes. When I laid my eyes on Teri, I said to myself,

"Fella, you are just about to cross the big boundary line." And I crossed it and there ain't a yellow rose in all of Texas who'll ever turn my heart like her.

CHIZUYE. *(Shoots a basket and misses; the other "men" kid him.)* I never even saw a Japanese until the war. I just fell in love with this strange girl. She happened to be Japanese, and she happened to be pretty ballsy and bright. She may be less Japanese now, but I think that's her way of survival. I hate to think what a loner I'd become without her, and vice versa.

ATSUKO. *(Mimics urinating with back turned to audience.)* Ats and I are a good example of opposites attracting, but she's the only person who calls me Kazuhiro ... just like my mom used to.

TERUKO. Aw, well ain't that cute. *(Teruko and Atsuko mimic tagging each other, shooting two baskets competitively.)*

TERUKO. Two points. Whoosh.

ATSUKO. *(Joking.)* Wimp. *(Shoots and revels in victory. Teruko and Atsuko do a quick "Three Stooges" exchange.)*

ATSUKO. Women. You can't live with 'em and —

HIMIKO. And you can't shoot 'em. Not anymore. Even though they're Japs *(Dark, reverberating laughter that disturbs the other "men.")*

ATSUKO. *(Approaches Himiko.)* Hamilton, I'm tired of hearing that word. What should I call you? White trash?

HIMIKO. I'm the only real American here. *(With pride.)* All-American mutt. *(More somberly, threateningly to Atsuko.)* Fightin' Japs ... marryin' Japs. Yellow skin and slit eyes. Just like the man in the jungle. Wanting me to die so he could live.

TERUKO. I remember the time your wife ran out of your house wearing a slip. She said you'd had a fight and you told her you wanted to kiss and make up. *(A pause as the others re-live this, too.)* And you kissed her, all right — and bit off part of her lip. They had to sew it back on.

HIMIKO. What can I say. There's nobody like her. Never has been. *(A pause.)* Never will be. She's the only prize I ever won. *(The others eye him like a jury and Himiko laughs.)*

SETSUKO. What did you expect, Hamilton? You'd bring her home and she'd sprout blue eyes and whistle "Dixie"?

HIMIKO. *(Anger simmering just under the surface and finally busting loose.)* Hey, what do you want me to do? Huh? She crawls under my fist like an orphan beggin' for love and my knuckles come down like a magnet, man. I got eight younger brothers and sisters and I lived in a trailer the size of a pencil box, working three jobs while you guys was jabbin' broads in the alley. Fuckin'-ay man, give me some room to breathe in. *(Himiko spins away as lights blackout on the "men." Spotlight simultaneously fades up on Chizuye.)*

CHIZUYE. Gustavo always said, "Chiz, you're gonna love Kansas. It's real slow, I know, but we'll have a house and a business, and Mama's going to spoil you rotten." He was going to teach me how to build a snowman, our project for that first winter in Kansas. So the snow came and we waited. He said it had to be just the right wetness so we could pack it tightly, so we could make a snowman who would outlive all other snowmen. A *perfect* snowman. That afternoon, Mama Juarez and I were making cinnamon-hot chocolate for when Gustavo came home. Snow was falling around the steaming window. The icy streets looked like a distorted mirror. And, somewhere where I couldn't hear him call, where he couldn't grab my hand for help, Gustavo was sliding into another world, thinking only of me as the ice cut into his beautiful face. The next day, the snow was perfect for building our snowman. But I didn't know how to build anything without Gustavo. And I told myself I would never not know how again. *(A pause, a vow to herself.)* Perfect. *(Setsuko enters the light and hovers over her.)*

SETSUKO. My youngest takes home economics. She taught me how to make cookie and milk. I'm almost done. The phone rings. "Mrs. Banks?" the army doctor says, "We regret to inform you Sergeant Banks passed away at fourteen hundred thirty-two hours." The nightmares of war had chased his heart away. *(A pause.)* The girls come home, their sloe-shaped eyes full of the sun. I ask them if they want to go "home" — to Japan. Or to California, where there are more *(Smiles.)* "Hybrid Japanese." They say they want to go with me. That I am home. And so, I have a family to raise and my house. I'm staying right here and I dare anyone to move me.

CHIZUYE. Setsuko. *(Chizuye holds onto her, a move that makes Setsuko uncomfortable at first but then becomes necessary for both of them.)*

SETSUKO. Yes.

CHIZUYE. *(With unbitter puzzlement.)* It wasn't perfect.

SETSUKO. But at least it was. At least we had it. Once. *(Lights dim on them with an immediate spotlight on Himiko.)*

HIMIKO. *(With quiet, determined dignity without a shred of anger or self-pity.)* No, we didn't. We never had it. All we had filtering through our fists was the powder left when a dream explodes in your face and your soul is left charred with the memory of what could have been if there was no war, if there was never a drink to help him forget, never a place like this where our dignity was tied to a tree and left hanging for strangers to spit on. *(Himiko exits as Chizuye and Setsuko return to the tatami room and lights cross-fade ...)*

Scene 4

Cold Tea

The women reflect exhaustion and contemplation. They appear to be sitting closer, except for Atsuko, who is distant both physically and psychologically.

SETSUKO. The tea is cold.

ATSUKO. Well, we must make a fresh pot. *(Exits to kitchen to do so.)*

TERUKO. We've been talking so much.

SETSUKO. Yes, things get cold when neglected.

TERUKO. *(Checks Atsuko's tea tin and calls out to Atsuko.)* We're out of your tea, Atsuko-san. May we drink "peasant" tea?

ATSUKO. *(From the kitchen.)* Have what you want. *(Atsuko returns with fresh hot water for tea.)*

TERUKO. I've been in Kansas so long, I don't know good tea from bad.

CHIZUYE. Oh, Teruko, come on. You've adjusted the best; you're an entrepreneur. You and Curt started from scratch: Japanese barber comes to Kansas.

TERUKO. Curtis wants to stay here. Maybe buy a farm. I think that's okay. Setchan, what about you? Do you think you'll marry again and stay here?

SETSUKO. If a nice man comes along ... maybe. I will be fine.

CHIZUYE. How many Kansas rednecks are there who can think of a Japanese as anything but a geisha or Tokyo Rose? Even the most beautiful Japanese in the world couldn't find a man for miles who'd see her as a real person. *(A pause.)* I don't want to love again. It hurts too much when they go away.

ATSUKO. Well, I suppose you all envy me, thinking I'm the lucky one. *(The women react to her again.)* But my husband promised he'd leave the army and we'd move to California. He's still in the army and we're still here. *(A pause.)* It's so unfair that I have to die in Kansas.

TERUKO. *(Tired of Atsuko's ridiculous fears.)* Atsuko-san, you're going to live a long time.

ATSUKO. So? What difference does it make? When we're dead, no one will remember there were Japanese in Kansas.

TERUKO. What will happen to the last one? Who will bury her?

ATSUKO. When it comes down to it, we're alone. Just like Himiko. She died alone.

SETSUKO. But she's not alone now. I am with her.

ATSUKO. Oh, spare me. She's dead. Who cares about death unless it's happening to you?

HIMIKO. They must care. If my journey leaves me stranded here, they, too, will have no passage.

TERUKO. I am with Himiko-san, too.

ATSUKO. Well, I'm not and I never was. *(Starts gathering her cup and goodies.)* In fact, I'm ready to go home. I've wasted my day and, let's face it, all the cleaning in the world isn't going to change Himiko's life or help her find a new life that's any better.

SETSUKO. Maybe it's really not Himiko's life you're worried about. Maybe it's yours, Atsuko-san. *(Atsuko looks outward. Her eyes lock with Himiko's for a moment. Himiko bows her head towards her invitingly. Atsuko shakes her head as if she has seen something and then turns to the women again.)*

ATSUKO. *(Uneasy and caustic.)* Come on. Let's be honest. Since when has anyone really cared about Himiko Hamilton? We've always known she was crazy. Poor Teruko, you had to live in the same neighborhood as her. You couldn't even go into your front yard without her bothering you. Of course, Himiko was scared of Chizuye so she didn't bother her too much. She admired you, Chizuye. Yes. You had become a model American. She used to talk about your "perfect American" accent. Said you sounded just like a television star.

CHIZUYE. Atsuko, shut up before I lose my temper. I've been saving it up for you all these years, so if it gets loose ...

TERUKO. *(Gently, again trying to deter confrontation.)* It *was* Chizuye who finally came to check on Himiko when she disappeared. She found her here. Sleeping.

CHIZUYE. Dead. For at least three days. To think of it.

SETSUKO. No. She died many years ago. Of a broken heart.

33

ATSUKO. Oh, you all make me laugh. Such tragedy in your eyes. I can just hear the shakuhachi playing in the background as you weep for her spirit.

SETSUKO. That's enough, Atsuko-san.

ATSUKO. Enough what? Enough laughter for the joke the war played on my life? Enough tears for having no allegiance except what I practice in the silence of my soul? Excuse me for not being strong like you, Setsuko. We all have our own problems to worry about. Maybe you think you can bear the weight of the world, but I can't.

CHIZUYE. What you can do for me is shut up. You've always been a mean, selfish bitch, Atsuko.

ATSUKO. *(Quite taken aback, tries to collect herself.)* Teruko, let's go! *(Teruko shakes her head firmly.)* Teruko!

TERUKO. *(Highly upset, the words spill out uncontrollably.)* Atsuko, I know you're afraid because the first of us is dead. Maybe you think soon we'll be having tea like this after you die. And maybe that is what will be. You can't control that. But you *can* control how you treat people.

SETSUKO. And the respect you owe the dead.

ATSUKO. Oh, just leave me alone. I wish I'd never come here today.

CHIZUYE. But we did, didn't we? Like the good Japanese ladies we are. *(A pause.)* We're not here because we have to be. Japanese manners don't require us to pay homage to some loon of a woman, even if she *was* Japanese. No, we're here today because we hurt inside like we never have before. Because when the first of us goes so violently and it's all over the papers, it wakes us up. For the first time in our lives, we gather together all the pieces of our used-up hearts and come running here hoping we'll find some kind of miracle that will glue it all back together and send us into our old age with something to hold onto.

TERUKO. But today we *have* all gone a little farther with each other than we ever have before.

CHIZUYE. Tomorrow it'll be status quo again.

SETSUKO. No, it won't ever be like it used to be again.

ATSUKO. Speak for yourself. *(A challenge, desperately trying to maintain the control she has always enjoyed over Teruko.)* Are you coming, Teruko? (She begins to move toward an exit; she is full of anger and suppressing tears. She turns once again to look at Teruko. Setsuko stands supportively behind Teruko. The words bite out of Atsuko's mouth.) Teruko ... this is your last chance. *(To her shock, Teruko even more firmly turns away. Devastated, Atsuko moves toward the*

34

*door and then, defeated, falls to her knees; Himiko immediately comes
to her side.)*

HIMIKO. Atsuko-san, stay. If you leave now, no one will rest.
*(Himiko stands in front of Atsuko and, without touching her, helps her
to stand and maintain using her hands as delicate guides. Atsuko fights
with herself and then turns back to the women. She bows in apology to
Teruko who bows back. She turns toward the door again, but Setsuko
bows to her. Feeling better, Atsuko returns the bow. Still uncomfortable, Atsuko glances at Chizuye who motions kindly for her to sit
down. She does and the other women follow suit, except for Teruko.)*

TERUKO. The only time we have taken tea together is whenever
something bad happened to a Japanese "war bride." We have the
best tea and realize how little we understand about each others'
choices in husbands, in raising our children, in whether or not we
choose to embrace America. Americans don't want us. Japanese
Americans too busy feeling bad themselves. We can't go back to
Japan. That's why I say family is the most important thing. What
makes us the most happiest? Our children. Our children. *(Chizuye
exits as lights cross-fade to the tatami area and music — perhaps
"Runaway" — fades up rapidly.* The women dance onto the tatami
area as young girls. The "girls" assume positions as if enjoying themselves
at a slumber party manicuring, Teruko rolling someone's hair, putting
on cosmetics, etc. Atsuko mimics smoking. The women are playing their
daughters. They sing the lyrics of the song and burst into laughter.)*

ATSUKO. Can you believe it? My mom won't let me go out for
cheerleading. She said it's too "sexual." *(Imitates mother's accent.)*
"Don't do skiing. Japanese don't ski. Don't do motorcycle. Don't do
skydive." She even thinks life insurance guarantees you don't die.
When I was born, she bought me a hundred-thousand dollar policy.

SETSUKO. My mother worries about life, not death. *(Imitates
mother's accent.)* "Did you eat your raw egg and fermented soy
beans today? Did you have bowel movement?" *(Laughs.)* Mom's so
funny. We were separated in a store and, over the intercom, I
heard "Japanese mother lost in dry goods. Will her daughter
please claim her?"

TERUKO. My mother doesn't worry about anything except my
dad. When she starts licking the bottom of his shoes and gets that
look in her eye, *(Mimics her mother doing this.)* I can say, "Mom,
hi, I'm going to join the Marines, become a lesbian, screw the foot-

* See Special Note on Songs and Recordings on copyright page.

35

ball team." She'd just say, *(Imitates mother's accent.)* "Okay, Linda. That's good. Have to fix dinner for sugar pie now."

ATSUKO. *(Does breast exercises.)* Man, the only thing that really bugs me after all these years is having to take my shoes off in the house.

SETSUKO. I thought I was going to die when my date picked me up for the homecoming dance. While he waited for me, my mother put shower caps over his shoes! *(Except for Himiko, the "girls" laugh and ad lib sounds of embarrassment. Himiko is eerily silent.)*

TERUKO. Mieko, what about *your* mother? *(Teruko cannot help giggling, although she tries hard to suppress it. It is contagious.)* She came to our house wearing that blonde wig. She slurped her tea and crocheted those green and purple poodle toilet paper covers. Ugh. *(All but Himiko laugh nervously, unable to restrain themselves, despite Himiko's cold stare.)*

HIMIKO. *(Without feeling, no sense of bitterness, with an eerie smile.)* I hate the world. *(Fresh laughter from the other "girls.")*

ATSUKO. So take a number, Mieko.

HIMIKO. You guys don't know anything about what life really is. Life is about relationships. Relationships with guys.

TERUKO. Oh, Mieko. We all date guys.

HIMIKO. It isn't about dating guys. It's about being *fucked* by guys. *(Their laughter is cut short by Himiko's remark. Their motions grind to a halt. Teruko in the middle of putting on lipstick, Atsuko in the middle of a laugh, and so on. They are shocked at this language and eye one another uncomfortably. Himiko seems to enjoy this power.)* By everybody: your mother, your father — and even yourself. *(A pause as she looks away from the girls and then she hits the table with the palm of her hand, frightening the other girls.)* Don't ask me about my mother. Because then you're asking me about myself ... and I don't know who the hell I am. *(She spins away from the other girls, moving to one side of the stage and folding herself into a ball and the other "girls" exit quickly. A light fades up on Himiko, now having reassumed the persona of the spirit.)* I was born in a storm and it's never stopped raining. My only blessing is Mieko, my half-Japanese girl. I love her so much, but she was born in my storm, too. For years, I tried to talk to her, but she wasn't ready. *(A sad laugh.)* Mieko is so fast, I only know what she looks like from behind. Because she's always leaving, her big Japanese o-shiri swaying like a flower, out looking for dreams she thinks men are going to give her. So it was a Saturday in May. Mieko wants to make me worry, so she *hitchhikes*.

She's gone three days. Then the big policeman comes. "Do you have a daughter named Mieko? When's the last time you saw her, Mrs. Hamilton?" *(Breathes hard and fast; forces composure.)* The last time I saw Mieko is in the dusk. She looks so Japanese, her shoulders curving like gentle hills. "Perfect kimono shoulders," her grandmother would say. *(A pause.)* Mieko came home today. Someone made her dirty, stabbed her in the chest many times and then raped her as she died. Left a broom inside my little girl's body. Her brassiere was shredded by the knife. *(A pause.)* There is no one for me; there never was. Even my sisters of Japan cannot bless me with sandals to cover my blistered feet as I prepare for the longest journey. *(Looks around.)* Billy, is that you? Before it's too late, tell me the truth. You loved me, didn't you? Once. Once there was nobody like me. Now that I know, I can go on without you, Billy. I see you there, waiting in the mist, your strong arms ready to hold me for one last dance. But I'm going another way. Like bamboo, I sway back and forth in the wind, bending but never breaking. Never again. The war is over. Mother? Is that you? Are you waiting for me, too? *(Brief, absolute delight, addressing Mieko when she was five.)* Mieko-chan, I see you dancing in my best kimono all light and laughter and ... clean! *(The delight fades.)* No, you all have to let me go now. I have a long walk ahead of me. All ties are unbound, as completely as if they never existed. *(She exits as lights dim and we bridge into the next scene. Wind chimes tinkle in the darkness:)*

Scene 5

Perfect Drinking Temperature

SETSUKO, ATSUKO, CHIZUYE and TERUKO. *(From various corners of the stage, they chant in the style of Buddhist chanting; in English the ancient poem means "I don't care/What anybody says./I will never stop/Loving you.")* Hito wa dono yo ni, i oo to mamayo.
SETSUKO. Tsunor'ya
ATSUKO. ... suru to mo ...
TERUKO. ... yami ...
CHIZUYE. ... wa senu.
SETSUKO. Hito wa dono yo ni ...

37

ATSUKO. ... i oo to mamayo ...

TERUKO. Tsunor'ya suru to mo ...

CHIZUYE. Yami wa senu.

SETSUKO. Himi-chan.

ATSUKO. Himiko.

TERUKO. Himiko-san.

CHIZUYE. Searching.

SETSUKO. For peace

TERUKO. Finally free.

CHIZUYE. Himiko-san. *(As if drawn to the power of their harmony, Himiko enters dressed in resplendent kimono. Moving gracefully, she comes center stage as the chanting continues.)*

SETSUKO. Your sisters call.

TERUKO. Come.

ATSUKO. Come unto us.

ALL. Come to tea with us. *(They study each other thoughtfully and then surround Himiko with warmth. Himiko kneels before them, facing the audience and bows her head low. A whisper:)* Gan'batte.

SETSUKO. *(A whisper in the shadow of "gan'batte.")* Perservere. *(The women return to the tatami room, wind chimes marking the transition. Himiko follows and watches them.)*

CHIZUYE. I am glad I came here today. Somehow, I feel at home with you women, you Japanese women. *(Smiles.)* Today.

SETSUKO. We should have let anyone who wanted to help come over. Today, even taking tea is different.

ATSUKO. Yes, even tea tastes different.

CHIZUYE. Maybe we will have tea again. All of us?

SETSUKO. Yes, Chizuye-san. Soon.

TERUKO. As you wish it.

SETSUKO. Atsuko-san?

ATSUKO. *(Looks around the room as if she senses a ghost; answers slowly.)* Yes? *(A frightened beat.)* Himiko is here, isn't she?

TERUKO. Oh, please, you're scaring me. Let's not talk about ghosts.

ATSUKO. But maybe that's the fate that awaits us all. A black space where the war dead and us, the war wounded, must sit out eternity.

SETSUKO. If it is our destiny, then—

CHIZUYE. Then it is our destiny.

TERUKO. So, ne.

SETSUKO. *(The women look solemnly at one another as Setsuko bows in honor of Himiko.)* Okagesama de.

CHIZUYE. *(Takes a cup for Himiko and acknowledges her.)* In your honorable shadow. *(Puts a fifth cup on the table.)* Please join us for tea. *(The women sit for a last drink of tea. Himiko joins them. They lift their cups simultaneously and slightly bow their heads to one another. Himiko forms a cup with her hands and drinks from it in unison with the others. She looks happier.)* HIMIKO. Perfect. *(The minute that word is uttered, the women pack up their things, ad lib farewells in Japanese — "sa," "ikimasho, ne," "mata, ne," "tsukaresama deshita," "ato de denwa shimasu," etc. — except for Chizuye. She is the last to speak and says "bye-bye" and Teruko responds with "bye-bye." They exit in different directions. Setsuko lingers as if trying to absorb Himiko's energy from the air. She bows deeply. Then she, too, exits as traditional Japanese music fades up. Taking each cup of tea and bowing to the woman who left the tea before, Himiko pours the remnants into her cup. She gathers strength from this and moves down stage center where she kneels. Holding the cup outward, she bows gracefully to the audience and then drinks the tea with extreme thirst that appears to be satisfied from the drink. She sets the cup down in front of her and smiles a half-smile, perhaps like that of Mona Lisa, to the audience. She bows low, all the way to the floor. Blackout.)*

End of Play

PROPERTY LIST

Pistol
Rayban Sunglasses
Long blonde wig
Piles of books
Wild-looking blonde wig
Cardigan sweater
Handkerchief
4 Japanese sitting cushions
Tea kettle
5 tea cups
Lacquer coasters
Wet cloth, dry cloth
Lacquer tray
Crocheted green and purple poodle toilet covers
Trunk
Wallet
Basket of food wrapped in *furoshiki*
Fruit and *makizushi*
Cigarette and lighter
Black bag
Can of beer
4 tins of tea
Photo album
Some fabrics
Jar of instant coffee
Spoons
Plates of food
Japanese fan
Kimonos

SOUND EFFECTS

Gunshot
Deafening atomic-like explosion
Smoke
Siren wail
Whistle of tea kettle
Tinkle of wind chimes

NEW PLAYS

★ **THE PICTURE OF DORIAN GRAY by Roberto Aguirre-Sacasa, based on the novel by Oscar Wilde.** Preternaturally handsome Dorian Gray has his portrait painted by his college classmate Basil Hallwood. When their mutual friend Henry Wotton offers to include it in a show, Dorian makes a fateful wish—that his portrait should grow old instead of him—and strikes an unspeakable bargain with the devil. [5M, 2W] ISBN: 978-0-8222-2590-4

★ **THE LYONS by Nicky Silver.** As Ben Lyons lies dying, it becomes clear that he and his wife have been at war for many years, and his impending demise has brought no relief. When they're joined by their children all efforts at a sentimental goodbye to the dying patriarch are soon abandoned. "Hilariously frank, clear-sighted, compassionate and forgiving." –*NY Times.* "Mordant, dark and rich." –*Associated Press.* [3M, 3W] ISBN: 978-0-8222-2659-8

★ **STANDING ON CEREMONY by Mo Gaffney, Jordan Harrison, Moisés Kaufman, Neil LaBute, Wendy MacLeod, José Rivera, Paul Rudnick, and Doug Wright, conceived by Brian Shnipper.** Witty, warm and occasionally wacky, these plays are vows to the blessings of equality, the universal challenges of relationships and the often hilarious power of love. "CEREMONY puts a human face on a hot button issue and delivers laughter and tears rather than propaganda." –*BackStage.* [3M, 3W] ISBN: 978-0-8222-2654-3

★ **ONE ARM by Moisés Kaufman, based on the short story and screenplay by Tennessee Williams.** Ollie joins the Navy and becomes the lightweight boxing champion of the Pacific Fleet. Soon after, he loses his arm in a car accident, and he turns to hustling to survive. "[A] fast, fierce, brutally beautiful stage adaptation." –*NY Magazine.* "A fascinatingly lurid, provocative and fatalistic piece of theater." –*Variety.* [7M, 1W] ISBN: 978-0-8222-2564-5

★ **AN ILIAD by Lisa Peterson and Denis O'Hare.** A modern-day retelling of Homer's classic. Poetry and humor, the ancient tale of the Trojan War and the modern world collide in this captivating theatrical experience. "Shocking, glorious, primal and deeply satisfying." –*Time Out NY.* "Explosive, altogether breathtaking." –*Chicago Sun-Times.* [1M] ISBN: 978-0-8222-2687-1

★ **THE COLUMNIST by David Auburn.** At the height of the Cold War, Joe Alsop is the nation's most influential journalist, beloved, feared and courted by the Washington world. But as the '60s dawn and America undergoes dizzying change, the intense political dramas Joe is embroiled in become deeply personal as well. "Intensely satisfying." –*Bloomberg News.* [5M, 2W] ISBN: 978-0-8222-2699-4

DRAMATISTS PLAY SERVICE, INC.
440 Park Avenue South, New York, NY 10016 212-683-8960 Fax 212-213-1539
postmaster@dramatists.com   www.dramatists.com

NEW PLAYS

★ **BENGAL TIGER AT THE BAGHDAD ZOO by Rajiv Joseph.** The lives of two American Marines and an Iraqi translator are forever changed by an encounter with a quick-witted tiger who haunts the streets of war-torn Baghdad. "[A] boldly imagined, harrowing and surprisingly funny drama." *–NY Times.* "Tragic yet darkly comic and highly imaginative." *–CurtainUp.* [5M, 2W] ISBN: 978-0-8222-2565-2

★ **THE PITMEN PAINTERS by Lee Hall, inspired by a book by William Feaver.** Based on the triumphant true story, a group of British miners discover a new way to express themselves and unexpectedly become art-world sensations. "Excitingly ambiguous, in-the-moment theater." *–NY Times.* "Heartfelt, moving and deeply politicized." *–Chicago Tribune.* [5M, 2W] ISBN: 978-0-8222-2507-2

★ **RELATIVELY SPEAKING by Ethan Coen, Elaine May and Woody Allen.** In TALKING CURE, Ethan Coen uncovers the sort of insanity that can only come from family. Elaine May explores the hilarity of passing in GEORGE IS DEAD. In HONEYMOON MOTEL, Woody Allen invites you to the sort of wedding day you won't forget. "Firecracker funny." *–NY Times.* "A rollicking good time." *–New Yorker.* [8M, 7W] ISBN: 978-0-8222-2394-8

★ **SONS OF THE PROPHET by Stephen Karam.** If to live is to suffer, then Joseph Douaihy is more alive than most. With unexplained chronic pain and the fate of his reeling family on his shoulders, Joseph's health, sanity, and insurance premium are on the line. "Explosively funny." *–NY Times.* "At once deep, deft and beautifully made." *–New Yorker.* [5M, 3W] ISBN: 978-0-8222-2597-3

★ **THE MOUNTAINTOP by Katori Hall.** A gripping reimagination of events the night before the assassination of the civil rights leader Dr. Martin Luther King, Jr. "An ominous electricity crackles through the opening moments." *–NY Times.* "[A] thrilling, wild, provocative flight of magical realism." *–Associated Press.* "Crackles with theatricality and a humanity more moving than sainthood." *–NY Newsday.* [1M, 1W] ISBN: 978-0-8222-2603-1

★ **ALL NEW PEOPLE by Zach Braff.** Charlie is 35, heartbroken, and just wants some time away from the rest of the world. Long Beach Island seems to be the perfect escape until his solitude is interrupted by a motley parade of misfits who show up and change his plans. "Consistently and sometimes sensationally funny." *–NY Times.* "A morbidly funny play about the trendy new existential condition of being young, adorable, and miserable." *–Variety.* [2M, 2W] ISBN: 978-0-8222-2562-1

DRAMATISTS PLAY SERVICE, INC.
440 Park Avenue South, New York, NY 10016 212-683-8960 Fax 212-213-1539
postmaster@dramatists.com www.dramatists.com

NEW PLAYS

★ **CLYBOURNE PARK by Bruce Norris.** WINNER OF THE 2011 PULITZER PRIZE AND 2012 TONY AWARD. Act One takes place in 1959 as community leaders try to stop the sale of a home to a black family. Act Two is set in the same house in the present day as the now predominantly African-American neighborhood battles to hold its ground. "Vital, sharp-witted and ferociously smart." –*NY Times.* "A theatrical treasure…Indisputably, uproariously funny." –*Entertainment Weekly.* [4M, 3W] ISBN: 978-0-8222-2697-0

★ **WATER BY THE SPOONFUL by Quiara Alegría Hudes.** WINNER OF THE 2012 PULITZER PRIZE. A Puerto Rican veteran is surrounded by the North Philadelphia demons he tried to escape in the service. "This is a very funny, warm, and yes uplifting play." –*Hartford Courant.* "The play is a combination poem, prayer and app on how to cope in an age of uncertainty, speed and chaos." –*Variety.* [4M, 3W] ISBN: 978-0-8222-2716-8

★ **RED by John Logan.** WINNER OF THE 2010 TONY AWARD. Mark Rothko has just landed the biggest commission in the history of modern art. But when his young assistant, Ken, gains the confidence to challenge him, Rothko faces the agonizing possibility that his crowning achievement could also become his undoing. "Intense and exciting." –*NY Times.* "Smart, eloquent entertainment." –*New Yorker.* [2M] ISBN: 978-0-8222-2483-9

★ **VENUS IN FUR by David Ives.** Thomas, a beleaguered playwright/director, is desperate to find an actress to play Vanda, the female lead in his adaptation of the classic sadomasochistic tale *Venus in Fur.* "Ninety minutes of good, kinky fun." –*NY Times.* "A fast-paced journey into one man's entrapment by a clever, vengeful female." –*Associated Press.* [1M, 1W] ISBN: 978-0-8222-2603-1

★ **OTHER DESERT CITIES by Jon Robin Baitz.** Brooke returns home to Palm Springs after a six-year absence and announces that she is about to publish a memoir dredging up a pivotal and tragic event in the family's history—a wound they don't want reopened. "Leaves you feeling both moved and gratifyingly sated." –*NY Times.* "A genuine pleasure." –*NY Post.* [2M, 3W] ISBN: 978-0-8222-2605-5

★ **TRIBES by Nina Raine.** Billy was born deaf into a hearing family and adapts brilliantly to his family's unconventional ways, but it's not until he meets Sylvia, a young woman on the brink of deafness, that he finally understands what it means to be understood. "A smart, lively play." –*NY Times.* "[A] bright and boldly provocative drama." –*Associated Press.* [3M, 2W] ISBN: 978-0-8222-2751-9

DRAMATISTS PLAY SERVICE, INC.
440 Park Avenue South, New York, NY 10016 212-683-8960 Fax 212-213-1539
postmaster@dramatists.com www.dramatists.com